Tell Me Why

WHY?

I Need Glasses

Jennifer Colby

Published in the United States of America by Cherry Lake Publishing
Ann Arbor, Michigan
www.cherrylakepublishing.com

Content Adviser: Charisse Gencyuz, M.D., Clinical Instructor, Department of Internal Medicine,
University of Michigan
Reading Adviser: Marla Conn, ReadAbility, Inc

Photo Credits: © KPG_Payless/Shutterstock Images, cover, 1, 9; © VannPhotography/Shutterstock Images,
cover, 1, 13; © Vicki L. Miller/Shutterstock Images, cover, 1, 21; © Olesya Feketa/Shutterstock Images, 5;
© wavebreakmedia/Shutterstock Images, 7; © baranq/Shutterstock Images, 11; © GRei/Shutterstock
Images, 13; © robertlamphoto/Shutterstock Images, 15; © Peter Bernik/Shutterstock Images, 19

Library of Congress Cataloging-in-Publication Data

Colby, Jennifer, 1971-
 I need glasses / Jennifer Colby.
    pages cm.—(Tell me why . . .)
 Includes index.
 Audience: 6–10
 Audience: Grade K to grade 3
 ISBN 978-1-63362-613-3 (hardcover)—ISBN 978-1-63362-793-2 (pdf)—
ISBN 978-1-63362-703-1 (pbk.)—ISBN 978-1-63362-883-0 (ebook)
 1. Eyeglasses—Juvenile literature. 2. Vision disorders—Juvenile literature. 3. Eye—Examination—
Juvenile literature. I. Title.

 RE976.C65 2015
 617.7'522—dc23

                              2014047989

Cherry Lake Publishing would like to acknowledge the work of the Partnership for 21st Century Skills.
Please visit www.p21.org for more information.

Printed in the United States of America
Corporate Graphics

Table of Contents

Everything Is So Fuzzy!

Eliza likes her classes at school. She always sits in the front row. That way she can see the whiteboard better than when she sits in the back. But lately the words on the board are fuzzier than usual. Why can't she read them?

Eliza rubs her eyes and **squints** at the board. That doesn't help. Maybe she's just been tired lately. But then one day, taking a spelling test, she realizes that all the letters just look like little smudges. Did she forget how to read? Or is something wrong with her eyes?

How many of your friends, teachers, or family members wear glasses?

Not being able to see well can make school difficult.

Eliza's teacher notices that her homework scores are dropping, and some of her answers seem to belong to different questions. She asks Eliza if she is having trouble reading the words on the page. The teacher wonders if Eliza might need glasses.

Children may need glasses for different reasons. A child's eyes are growing and **developing**. Glasses may help a child's eyes grow in a healthy way. A child may need glasses to help her see clearly. Sometimes a child's eyes are crossed. Sometimes one eye is weaker than the other.

Do you have trouble reading? Ask your teacher or parent if you need to have your eyes checked.

A teacher might be able to help you figure out if bad eyesight is why you have trouble reading.

Glasses can help protect eyes from **damage** caused by working too hard. People who need glasses but don't have them may get lots of headaches.

For someone with poor vision, getting glasses helps them with many different things. Besides making reading easier, glasses can help you see facial expressions more clearly. They can help with sports, letting you see when a ball is coming towards you. They can also help with activities like sewing or piano, which both require strong **hand-eye coordination**.

If you get glasses after needing them for a long time, it can feel life-changing.

The Eye Exam

Eliza's mom takes her to an **optometrist** to get her eyes checked. The optometrist is an eye expert. She will examine Eliza's eyes and let her know if she needs glasses.

The doctor puts special drops in Eliza's eyes. They do not hurt. These drops relax the eye muscle. Then the doctor can use a special instrument called a retinoscope to measure Eliza's **vision**. The doctor also asks Eliza questions about what she can and cannot see.

An optometrist uses machines to test patients' vision.

The eye doctor tells Eliza that she needs glasses. She writes a **prescription** for the glasses. Special **corrective lenses** will be made for Eliza to help her see better.

Eliza and her mom go to a store to pick out her new glasses. Eliza can choose from many different frames. The corrective lenses fit into the frames. She chooses a pair of bright purple frames.

Usually, people getting glasses are able to choose their own frames.

A Fashionable Fix

There are four reasons why someone might need glasses.

Myopia (nearsightedness) is a **condition** where someone cannot see things that are far away. Hyperopia (farsightedness) is a condition where things close-up are fuzzy. With astigmatism, someone's eye is shaped like a football instead of like a round basketball. Sometimes the eyes each see differently. This leads to a condition called amblyopia. When this happens, one eye does not develop normally.

NORMAL VISION AND MYOPIA

NORMAL VISION
FARAWAY OBJECT IS CLEAR

MYOPIA
NEARSIGHTED EYE
THE EYEBALL IS TOO LONG
FARAWAY OBJECT IS BLURRY

MYOPIA CORRECTED
CORRECTION WITH
A MINUS LENS

LOOK!

Reread the first chapter, then look at this diagram. Why do you think Eliza needs glasses? Is she nearsighted or farsighted?

The first eye shows normal vision. The second eye shows nearsightedness. The third eye shows nearsightedness that has been corrected.

Have you been given a prescription for glasses? If so, it is important that you wear them. Otherwise, your eyes might not grow the correct way. That can **permanently** damage your eyes.

Lots of people wear glasses. They are often stylish. Some people even have a couple pairs that they can switch with their outfits. Never be ashamed or nervous to wear your glasses. Wearing your glasses will help you do the things you want to do.

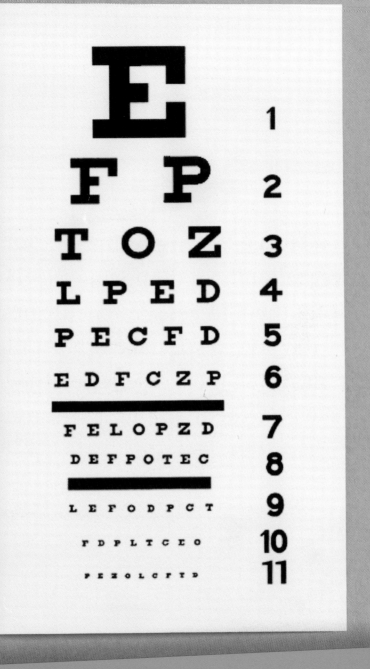

Optometrists point at letters and ask patients to say what they are. The smaller the letters, the harder it gets.

17

Caring for Glasses

Eliza needs to take care of her glasses.

She never takes them off during the day. She does not want them to get scratched. She cleans them every day with a special cloth. At night she places her glasses in their case. Then they will be safe until she puts them on in the morning.

People who wear glasses need to take good care of them. But don't rub the lenses on your clothing—only use the special cleaning cloths.

Eliza goes to the optometrist every year to get her eyes checked. The doctor uses the same tool to measure her vision. The doctor may need to write a new prescription for lenses. If so, Eliza can choose new frames. And when she's older, she might be able to get **contact lenses**.

Eliza loves her new glasses. Now she can read what the teacher writes on the board without squinting!

Glasses can make a unique fashion statement.

Think About It!

Do you think your eye color affects your vision? Why or why not? Go online with an adult to find the answer.

Cover one eye and try to read this page. Now uncover it and cover your other eye. Do you notice that one side is stronger?

Find someone you know who wears glasses. Ask them how long they've had them. How did they know they needed to get their eyes tested? What was it like to visit the optometrist? What is the best part of having glasses? What is the most challenging part?

Glossary

condition (kuhn-DISH-uhn) a medical problem that lasts for a long time

contact lenses (KAHN-takt lenzez) small plastic lenses that you wear on your eyeball to improve your vision

corrective (kuh-REK-tiv) having the power to make something right

damage (DAM-ij) the harm caused by something

developing (di-VEL-up-ing) growing

hand-eye coordination (HAND eye KOHR- duh-NAY-shun) the way that your hands and sight work together so you are able to do things that require speed and accuracy (such as catching or hitting a ball)

lenses (LENZ-iz) clear, curved pieces of glass

myopia (my-OH-pee-uh) a condition where someone can't see things that are far away

optometrist (ahp-TAH-muh-trist) a person who is licensed to test your vision and prescribe glasses or contact lenses

permanently (PIRM-uh-nuhnt-lee) lasting forever

prescription (pri-SKRIP-shuhn) an order for drugs, medicine, or glasses written by a doctor

squints (SKWINTS) looks at someone or something with one or both eyes partly closed, in an attempt to see more clearly

vision (VIZH-uhn) the sense of sight

Find Out More

Books:

Ballard, Carol. *Why Do I Need Glasses? Vision*. Chicago, Heinemann-Raintree, 2011.

Salzberg, Barney. *Arlo Needs Glasses*. New York: Workman Publishing Company, 2012.

Web Sites:

CDC—Kids' Quest: Vision Impairment
www.cdc.gov/ncbddd/kids/vision.html
Read about what it's like to be visually impaired.

Kids' Health: Eyes—Wearing Glasses
www.cyh.com/HealthTopics/HealthTopicDetailsKids.aspx?p=335&np=152&id=1826
Look at these tips from others kids about the best ways to adjust to wearing glasses, including how to deal with bullies.

Index

About the Author

Jennifer Colby did not need glasses as a child, but she does now. She lives in Michigan with her three children. She is a school librarian and loves to help students find the information they are looking for.